10. Jan is a waitress. She needs to improve her ability to listen to customers. What attitude should she take toward her coworkers' suggestions?

    a. She should listen only to the ideas that agree with her own.

    b. She should not pay attention to suggestions made by coworkers that are not good.

    c. She should listen to all the other coworkers' observations and evaluate them.

## Preview Chart

This chart will show you what skills you need to study. Reread each question you missed. Then look at the appropriate lesson of the book for help in understanding the correct answer.

| Question<br>Check the questions you missed. | Skill<br>The exercise, like the book, focuses on the skills below. | Lesson<br>Preview what you will learn in this book. |
| --- | --- | --- |
| 1. _____ | Evaluating your performance | 2 |
| 2. _____ | Being self-motivated | 1 |
| 3. _____ | Building a network | 6 |
| 4. _____ | Overcoming fears of failure | 8 |
| 5. _____ | Avoiding deadline stress | 7 |
| 6. _____ | Accepting and handling responsibility | 9 |
| 7. _____ | Building a positive self-image | 5 |
| 8. _____ | Being an asset to your company | 10 |
| 9. _____ | Working with others; being a team player | 3 |
| 10. _____ | Using negative feedback effectively | 4 |

P9-CPY-425

# Meeting Employer Expectations

What qualities do you think most employers want to see in employees?

What does being responsible mean to you?

How do you show honesty and integrity in the workplace?

Employers expect their employees to be responsible, honest, and self-motivated.

All employers want employees who are good at their jobs. But being good at a job takes more than just knowing how to do a task or perform a service well. It also requires certain personal qualities. Successful employees have a sense of responsibility in their jobs. They have honesty and integrity. In this lesson you will learn about the personal qualities that employers expect from employees.

## Show a Sense of Responsibility

Being **responsible** in the workplace means being able to be depended on to do your job. You are responsible if you can account for or answer for your actions. If you are responsible, people can count on you.

Many factors affect the assignments you receive. Your technical skills are one factor. Your personal qualities also play a role. If you show responsibility, you will be trusted with more tasks. One way to show responsibility is to complete your job assignments on time and well. If you can handle your main job tasks, you may be given additional tasks. You will earn the respect of both coworkers and supervisors if you show responsibility. Read the following case study for an example of a responsible employee.

## Case Study

Carl is an apprentice with Ace Plumbing and Electric. He is learning the basic skills to become a licensed plumber. He works with his supervisor, Angie, who is an expert in pipe fitting. Today Carl is supposed to have the day off. But Angie calls him at nine o'clock in the morning.

You can show a sense of responsibility by performing job tasks well and on time.

Angie: Listen, I know it's your day off. But I'm working on one of the labs in that chemical company on Janson Street. I really think this would be a good chance for you to try installing some glass pipes.

Carl: Yeah, I've been wanting to learn to work with glass pipes. Sure, I'll come in.

Angie: That's great, Carl. Can you be here in fifteen minutes?

Carl: I can do better than that. Janson Street is just two blocks from where I live. Why don't I meet you there?

Carl accepts the extra responsibility his supervisor offers him. Carl wants to gain more skill in his job. From just this brief conversation, Angie sees that Carl is willing to accept extra tasks. He has a good attitude and he's flexible. Angie is likely to give him more job responsibility in the future.

## Demonstrate Integrity and Honesty

Employers need to be able to depend on their employees. Obviously this means they must trust workers not to steal or lie. But it also means they must be comfortable giving employees a certain amount of responsibility. Employers look for workers who are honest and have integrity. To have **integrity** means to have a solid sense of what is the right thing to do. The following case study shows an employee who has integrity.

### — Case Study

Jolene works as a receptionist in a law firm. Her friend Bob calls her one afternoon and asks her to bring him a box of pens and a stapler from work.

Jolene: Bob, you know I can't do that. That's stealing.

Bob: Nobody will know. Just put them in a paper bag or something when you leave. It's a big company. They won't miss a few pens and a stapler. Come on. I really need that stuff.

Jolene: I'm not going to do that. I'm disappointed in you for even asking me.

Your employer needs to be able to trust you.

Jolene's employers will probably never know about her conversation with Bob. However, Jolene has proved that she is honest. She also has integrity. Even if she could steal the office supplies without getting caught, she chooses not to betray the trust that the company has in her. All employers expect their employees to be honest and to have integrity.

## Be Self-Motivated

Employers look for workers who are self-motivated. To be **self-motivated** means to drive yourself to act on your own and be a "self-starter." To be self-motivated means to act or perform without being asked to act. Self-motivated employees are enthusiastic about their work. They seek more responsibility on the job. They are excited to learn as much as they can about the work they do.

## Practice Self-Management

Being self-motivated is one part of self-management. If you practice **self-management,** you monitor or keep track of your behavior and performance. If you motivate yourself to complete goals, you are practicing self-management. Assessing your skills and making new goals to improve are also parts of self-management. Being responsible and self-motivated is the first step to succeeding in any career.

For example, suppose you work as a salesperson in a car dealership. Greeting customers is the first step in making a sale. You demonstrate that you are self-motivated by greeting customers who walk into the showroom. Your supervisor and coworkers do not need to tell you to greet customers. You may practice self-management by setting a goal for the number of cars you will try to sell by the end of the week or month. You might also assess or check how you are performing. Are there ways you could improve? Should you set different goals?

Showing responsibility and demonstrating integrity and honesty are qualities that are necessary in every workplace. Being self-motivated and practicing self-management are qualities that you can always improve.

# Comprehension Check

Complete the following exercises. Refer to the lesson if necessary.

**A. List what it means to show responsibility.**

_____

_____

_____

**B. Complete each sentence. Circle the letter in front of the answer.**

1. An employee who has honesty and integrity
   a. thinks it is acceptable to take home small items from the company.
   b. thinks that stealing is wrong.
   c. avoids responsibility.

2. Self-motivated employees
   a. act without being asked to act.
   b. refuse to do more than is required.
   c. do their best work alone.

3. Practicing self-management means
   a. refusing to do more than is required.
   b. setting goals and being self-motivated.
   c. learning only what is necessary.

4. A responsible worker does not
   a. complete assignments on time.
   b. earn the respect of coworkers.
   c. turn in incomplete work.

5. A worker who does not have integrity
   a. knows what is the right thing to do.
   b. is valued by employers.
   c. may take office supplies for personal use.

Answer the questions following each case. Then talk about your answers with your partner or group.

**Case A**

Elena works at Alegra Foods Supermarket. Recently, Elena's manager asked her to manage the store's salad bar. Elena has new responsibilities. She sets up the salad bar every morning. It has fifty different ingredients and each ingredient must go in a special place. Elena keeps a close eye on the salad bar throughout the day. She makes sure that the ingredients look clean and fresh. She restocks the salad bar when necessary. At the end of her shift, she must take all the ingredients to the storage cooler. Then she cleans the empty salad bar. Elena is glad the manager promoted her.

1. Name two personal qualities from the lesson that Elena needs to perform her new job task.

   _____

2. What might happen if Elena did not have these personal qualities?

   _____

   _____

**Case B**

Michael is an emergency medical technician (EMT). He works with a paramedic to assist people who need medical help. Each day the paramedic and the EMT check the supplies on the truck. They also make sure the equipment is working. Without the proper supplies and equipment, they may not be able to help the patients.

When they arrive at the scene of a medical emergency, the EMTs work together to figure out each patient's condition. Sometimes the EMTs have to perform life-saving procedures before they can move the patient. After an emergency call, the paramedic or the EMT prepares paperwork for the hospital or emergency office.

1. List the responsibilities for the medical team.

_____

_____

2. What might happen if the team was not responsible?

_____

_____

**Case C**

Winston is a camera technician for Oliver Studios. He prepares the equipment that is used by camera operators. He is gaining extra experience by volunteering for tasks that aren't part of his everyday work. He set a goal to learn as much as he can from the operators. The camera operators he works for are impressed with him. Sometimes they show him camera techniques. Winston is trying to learn as much as he can. Someday he would like to become a camera operator and work on movies.

1. Which skill from the lesson does Winston have?

_____

2. How is this skill helpful to Winston's long-term goals?

_____

_____

### TALK IT OUT

Work with a partner. Think of four different jobs. For each of the jobs, write an example of a worker using one of the personal qualities from the lesson: sense of responsibility, self-management, honesty and integrity, or self-motivation. You may find that some of your examples involve more than one skill.

# Think and Apply

How well do you use the skills in this lesson? Complete these exercises.

**A. Think about what you learned in this lesson and answer the questions. Share your answers with your partner or your class.**

1. Think about your job or a job you had in the past. Do you think you used the skills in this lesson on the job? If so, which skills? If not, why not?

   _____

2. Ask a friend to give you feedback about your skills and personal qualities. Tell the person to be as honest as possible. Ask the person to rate you from 1 (lowest) to 5 (highest) in the following areas: sense of responsibility; honesty and integrity; self-management; and relating to others. Do you agree with your friend's rating? Why or why not?

   _____

**B. Review your answers to A. Complete the checklist. Then answer the questions that follow.**

1. Read the list of skills and personal qualities. Check the boxes next to your strengths.
   - ☐ showing responsibility
   - ☐ demonstrating integrity and honesty
   - ☐ being self-motivated
   - ☐ practicing self-management

2. Do you want to improve any of your skills? Which ones?

   _____

   _____

3. How do you plan to improve the skills you listed in question 2?

   _____

   _____

# Practicing Self-Assessment

What is self-assessment?

Why is self-assessment a good idea?

Knowing how to assess or rate your own performance will help you improve your job skills.

No matter where you work, your coworkers and bosses will assess or check your performance. A coworker may ask you to correct your math on a financial report. Your boss may ask you to improve your writing skills. At times it will be important for you to check and review your performance yourself. **Self-assessment** is a way for you to check your performance and rate your skills. This lesson will present methods to help you review and evaluate your performance.

## Understand What's Expected of You

Being effective in the workplace means understanding the job requirements. It means knowing what's expected of you. Check the employee handbook to find your company's rules. This book may also contain advice about how to do your job. In any job, first learn to do the tasks that make up your job description. Also learn how your company expects you to handle your job tasks. Your supervisor will help you understand company rules. It's important to do your work according to the rules.

## Monitor Your Performance as You Work

To be a successful employee, learn to monitor your work performance. That means you must be aware of the job you are doing. Ask yourself, "How am I doing?" If you think you are doing well in every area of your job, give yourself a pat on the back. But be honest. Most people can find some areas in which they could improve. For example, suppose that you find it difficult to get along with coworkers or customers. Is the problem coming from you? Is there something you can do to improve? Whether the problem comes from you or someone else, take steps to change the situation. The following case study gives an example of when it would be useful to monitor job performance.

Concentrate on learning the tasks your job requires.

## Case Study

Natalie is a retail sales associate for a women's clothing store. She helps customers find the sizes, colors, and brand names they want. Lately, Natalie has noticed that customers don't seem to want her help. For example, a customer comes into the store and begins looking through a rack of dresses. Natalie approaches the customer and stands a couple of feet away watching her. After a moment or two the customer looks up.

Natalie: Hello. Is there something I can help you find?

Customer: No, thanks. I'm just looking.

Natalie: Bathing suits are 20 percent off this week.

Customer: I *said* I'm just looking.

The customer quickly walks away from Natalie. What annoyed the customer? Natalie needs to think about how she has treated this customer. She needs to ask herself what might be causing the problem. She needs to think about what customers say to her. By checking her behavior and performance, she becomes aware of a problem. Her next step will be to address the problem and try to correct her performance.

## Evaluate Your Performance

Monitoring your performance will help only if you follow it up with an evaluation. Sometimes it helps to make a self-rating sheet. A **self-rating sheet** is a tool for grading your own performance. Write out a list of your job tasks. Then rate the way you perform those tasks. You might use a rating system with numbers. The number 1 means "needs improvement," 2 means "OK," and 3 means "good." Make sure your answers are honest, or you will miss areas you need to improve. Pay special attention to the areas where you think you might be able to improve. If you think the problem is too big to handle alone, you might ask for input from a coworker or supervisor. In the following case study, Natalie evaluates her performance and figures out a way to improve.

### Case Study

Natalie isn't sure what she's doing wrong, but she knows there's a problem. She rereads the "Customer Service" section of her employee handbook. This section gives tips about how she should greet customers. She also reviews her notes from her interview and sales training class. Then she writes a self-rating sheet to assess her own performance. By asking herself questions about her own service skills, Natalie is able to identify the problem. She greets each customer courteously. However, she's been standing too close to them.

The employee handbook tells her that customers don't like salespeople "hovering over them." Natalie decides to change her behavior right away.

When the next customer comes in, Natalie is hanging up some blouses. She turns and smiles at the customer but doesn't move toward her. Natalie says hello. She asks the customer if she needs help finding anything. The customer thanks Natalie but says she is just looking. Natalie informs the customer of the sale on bathing suits and gives the customer her name if she needs anything.

Evaluating your performance can help you improve your customer service skills.

Natalie gave this customer all the information she'd given her earlier customers, but this time the customer felt comfortable. By monitoring her performance she has identified a problem. Rechecking her handbook and notes helps her review her responsibilities. After evaluating her sales technique, she identifies her mistake. She knows she can improve on her mistake by approaching customers differently. Natalie's self-assessment helps her improve her sales skills.

The self-assessment steps will take some time to complete. Allow yourself time to completely understand your tasks. Then decide on an amount of time for monitoring and evaluating. You might decide to monitor your tasks over a two-week or two-month period. After you evaluate your performance, you can set goals to improve your skills.

# Comprehension Check

Complete the following exercises. Refer to the lesson if necessary.

**A. List the three steps of self-assessment.**

1. _____

2. _____

3. _____

**B. What is a self-rating sheet?**

_____

**C. Mark the following statements T (True) or F (False).**

_____ 1. As you monitor your work, you become aware of your performance.

_____ 2. To evaluate your performance effectively, you need to be honest with yourself.

_____ 3. You do not need to understand your job tasks to assess your work.

**D. Complete each sentence. Circle the letter in front of the correct answer.**

1. Self-assessment is a way to

   a. check your job performance and rate your skills.
   b. be honest.
   c. understand what your company expects of you in your job.

2. If you need help to understand your work tasks, you can

   a. discuss the tasks with your supervisor.
   b. go ahead and do the work even if you don't understand.
   c. wait a while and see if you understand.

3. The first step in self-assessment is

   a. filling out a self-rating sheet.
   b. monitoring your performance.
   c. understanding what's expected of you.

# Making Connections

Answer the questions following each case. Then talk about your answers with your partner or group.

**Case A**

Adalia is a receptionist at Delivery Central, a package delivery company. She answers the telephone, schedules deliveries, and communicates with the company's 150 drivers. Once in a while, she gets a walk-in customer. Usually these people have many questions. Adalia is often so busy with the phone that she has little time for her walk-in customers. One day a customer comes in and has to wait ten minutes for Adalia to help him. She doesn't speak to him but keeps holding up her finger and signaling him to wait. When she is about to speak to the customer, he gets up and leaves the office without a word.

1. List some items you might include on a self-rating sheet for Adalia.

   _____

   _____

2. What might a self-rating sheet show Adalia?

   _____

   _____

**Case B**

Antoine works at a theme park. He greets all the customers who buy tickets to ride the Thrills Aplenty roller coaster. He takes their tickets and helps them onto the ride. He gives each rider a short speech on safety. There has never been an accident on this roller coaster. But people must be told how to sit in their seats correctly. Antoine knows that if he explains the ride to customers in the correct way, they shouldn't have any questions. He explains the instructions for the ride. He asks if everyone understands. The customers say *yes* and nod. He asks if they have questions. They say *no*.

How does Antoine monitor his ability to give instructions?

_____

_____

**Case C**

Ahmad is a nurse's assistant. He has patients all over the city. He travels to ten different homes each day. Each of his patients has a different medical condition. Ahmad handles each patient the same way. Because he has to see a lot of patients, he tries to get in and out as quickly as possible. Whenever Ahmad has to speak to a patient, he does so in a very loud voice. He also speaks very slowly. Lately he has begun to notice that all his patients are cranky. They don't seem to like him. He figures that's just the way sick people are. When his supervisor asks him how the job is going, Ahmad replies, "Just fine. No problems."

1. Do you think Ahmad has assessed his job performance accurately? Tell why.

_____

2. What clues might Ahmad use to assess his performance?

_____

_____

### ACT IT OUT

Work with a partner. One of you will be an employee of a clothing store or fast-food restaurant. The other will be a customer. The customer will order food or complain about something. The employee will respond. Afterward, the employee will write a self-evaluation. The customer will write an evaluation of the employee's service. Compare the two evaluations. Then switch roles and repeat the activity.

# Think and Apply

How well do you use the skills in this lesson? Complete these exercises.

**A. Think about what you learned in this lesson and answer the questions. Share your answers with your partner or your class.**

1. Think about a job that you have had or a project that you worked on at home or at school. What was expected of you? Did you monitor your performance? Did you evaluate your performance? Why or why not?

   _____

   _____

2. Talk to a friend about your experience. Discuss what you could have done or what you could do in the future to monitor and evaluate your performance. Write your ideas.

   _____

   _____

**B. Review your answers to A. Complete the checklist. Then answer the questions that follow.**

1. Read the list of skills. Check the boxes next to your strengths.

   ☐ understanding the tasks I'm assigned to do

   ☐ monitoring my job performance

   ☐ evaluating my performance

   ☐ creating and completing a self-rating sheet

2. Do you want to improve any of your skills? Which ones?

   _____

   _____

3. How do you plan to improve the skills you listed in question 2?

   _____

   _____

# Working with Others: Being a Team Player

What does teamwork mean to you?

What personal qualities do you need to be able to work with others?

Why do you think that teamwork is important to employers?

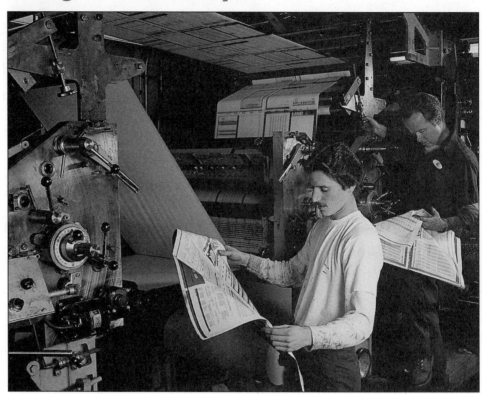

Employers expect their employees to be able to work together in order to accomplish necessary goals.

Today's employees need to know how to work as members of a team. **Teamwork** means individuals sharing ideas and efforts to accomplish a group goal. But there's more to teamwork than that. Teamwork requires some special personal qualities. You need to be able to take personal responsibility for your group's tasks. You must encourage other team members and help solve problems and arguments. Also, you must be able to work both as a leader and as a group member.

### Take Responsibility for Individual and Group Tasks

No team will work well if its members don't do what they promise to do. The best teams succeed because team members take responsibility and follow through. To **follow-through** means to complete the work of the team. Following through sometimes requires volunteering for group tasks.

It's important to remember that the work you do represents your whole team. You are part of a larger group effort that requires individual effort and responsibility. If the team fails to meet a goal, each member is responsible for not meeting the goal.

## Resolve Disputes

Disputes or disagreements occur in every work group. Not everyone agrees all the time. Every member brings a different point of view. One of the reasons for working as a team is to look at group tasks from more than one point of view. If the team is to be effective, disagreements must be handled carefully. During a disagreement in your group, the members need to listen carefully. Also, you need to remain open-minded, which means being willing to listen to the opinions of others.

Keep an open mind when you listen to a coworker's point of view.

To communicate well, team members also need to take responsibility for their own emotions. That means each individual must avoid losing his or her temper. There are ways to avoid the emotion and focus on settling or **resolving** the dispute. The following case study shows how a dispute can be resolved.

## Case Study

Jolene and Montell work at a small bakery called The Doughnut Whole. Jolene serves customers at the front counter and takes telephone orders. Montell works in the back as a baker. Today there was a communication problem between the two workers. Jolene takes a telephone order for twelve "bear claw" doughnuts. She walks to the baking area and calls out the order. Montell hears her and begins to make the bear claws. When he's finished, he boxes them up and brings them out to Jolene. To Jolene's surprise, Montell has baked twelve dozen bear claws. When she asks Montell about it, Montell loses his temper and tells Jolene that she ordered twelve dozen. Jolene denies it.

Jolene: The main thing is we have to figure out how to keep this from happening in the future.

Montell: It won't happen again if you put the order in the right way.

Jolene: I *did* put it in the right way, Montell.

Montell: Okay, I guess we should stop arguing about who's right and who's wrong. Could you write down each order and hand it to me when you tell me the order?

Jolene: That's fine with me.

Montell: But what are we going to do with all these bear claws? Throw them out?

Jolene: It would be a shame for them to go to waste after all your work. I know—we can run a special today. Two bear claws for the price of one.

At first, Montell loses his temper when Jolene tells him she only wanted twelve bear claws. But then he realizes that arguing will not solve anything. Instead, he and Jolene work together to solve the problem.

## Show Leadership

Sometimes, you may need to take the lead for your group. For example, if you have a talent or skill that no one else in the group has, you may be asked to teach that skill to the other members of your group.

**Leadership** means solving problems and guiding others. Read the following case study for an example of an employee showing leadership.

## Case Study

Raheem is a 911 emergency dispatcher. He takes emergency telephone calls. He serves as a link between victims of emergency situations and the hospitals or police officers who can help them. This job requires quick thinking and strong communication skills. This week Raheem is training a new employee, Maile. One night a woman calls in to report a reckless driver. The woman is calling from her car phone. The reckless driver is just ahead of her on the highway. Raheem keeps the woman on the phone while he calls the police. By going back and forth from the woman to the police officer, Raheem is able to get directions and tell the officer where the reckless driver is. Raheem stays in contact with the officer until the officer pulls the reckless driver over. Afterward, Raheem speaks with his trainee. He tells her that dispatchers work as part of a team. He explains that he and the caller and the police officer worked together to solve the problem of the reckless driver.

Emergency dispatchers need to speak clearly and demonstrate leadership.

Being a team player is a great responsibility. Your team members will rely on you to do your part and you will rely on them. Being part of a work team is also rewarding. Just as you take pride in your individual successes, you can share in the successes of your work team.

# Comprehension Check

Complete the following exercises. Refer to the lesson if necessary.

**A. List three personal qualities you need to be a good team member.**

1. _____

2. _____

3. _____

**B. List two communication skills you need in order to solve team disputes.**

1. _____

2. _____

**C. Complete each sentence. Circle the letter in front of the answer.**

1. When you follow through, you

    a. act to complete what you say you will do.
    b. blame others.
    c. tell other people what to do.

2. Disagreements

    a. can always be avoided.
    b. should be handled without emotion if possible.
    c. are not common in work groups.

3. To resolve his dispute with Jolene about the bear claws, Montell had to

    a. take responsibility for his own emotions.
    b. figure out who was right and who was wrong.
    c. ask a manager for help with the problem.

4. Showing leadership sometimes means

    a. working by yourself to achieve a group goal.
    b. teaching a skill to other members of your group.
    c. asking a coworker what to do to solve a problem.

## Making Connections

Answer the questions following each case. Then talk about your answers with your partner or group.

### Case A

Maya is a teacher's aide at Mount Pleasant Elementary School. Her duties include helping the teachers grade tests and homework. She also helps the teacher set up any audiovisual equipment, such as VCRs and film projectors. On Tuesday, the sixth-grade class is scheduled to watch a short film. When Maya gets to the classroom, she sees that the teacher, Mr. Elliott, is busy with a student. Maya looks at the clock. The class is supposed to begin in ten minutes. Maya waves to Mr. Elliott and then begins setting up the film projector. By the time all the students have arrived, Maya has finished setting up the projector. The class is ready to start.

As part of the teaching team with Mr. Elliott, what teamwork skills does Maya show?

_____

_____

_____

### Case B

Les is a soil conservation technician. His job requires him to design ways to maintain farm soil. He works with farmers to build irrigation systems. He also shows farmers how to avoid soil erosion problems. Today Les is working with Mandi and Gail, who are also technicians. They are visiting a farm to evaluate the soil. The group has three tasks today. The group needs to collect ten soil samples, check the water supply for the area, and collect ten water samples from the river.

Mandi: I'll collect the water samples from the river.

Gail: I'll drive over to the other end of the farm and gather the soil samples.

1. Describe what Gail and Mandi do for their group.

_____

_____

2. What should Les do to help the group?

_____

_____

## TRY IT OUT

Work in small groups. You will work together to build a model tower out of things that you have with you and things that you find in the classroom. Before you begin building your tower, discuss your team goals. Do you want to build the tallest tower in the classroom? Would you rather build the strongest tower or the most beautiful tower?

After you finish building your tower, each team will explain its goals and show its tower to the class. Choose one person to tell about your tower and how you built it. Then let the rest of the class ask questions about the tower and the building process. The class should ask your team how each member took responsibility for the tower, how you resolved disputes, and whether any team members showed leadership. Each team member should participate during the question-and-answer period.

# Think and Apply

How well do you use the skills in this lesson? Complete these exercises.

**A. Think about what you learned in this lesson and answer the questions. Share your answers with your partner or your class.**

1. Think about a time when you had to work in a small group at work, at school, or somewhere else. Did each team member add something to the process? Did team members encourage one another? Were there disagreements?

   _____

   _____

2. Share a story with a friend about working as a member of a team. Tell about how the team handled group goals, disagreements, and individual responsibility. Then have your friend share a story about working on a team. How would you describe your friend's teamwork skills? Explain your answer.

   _____

   _____

**B. Review your answers to A. Complete the checklist. Then answer the questions that follow.**

1. Read the list of teamwork skills. Check the boxes next to your strengths.

   ☐ taking responsibility for individual and group goals

   ☐ following through on group goals

   ☐ working to resolve disputes

   ☐ showing leadership

   ☐ working as both a leader and a group member

2. Do you want to improve any of your skills? Which ones?

   _____

3. How do you plan to improve the skills you listed in question 2?

   _____

# Accepting Positive and Negative Feedback

What are some examples of positive feedback?

What is negative feedback?

How can negative feedback help you?

Accepting positive and negative feedback in an appropriate way can help you be a better employee.

Praise and criticism are types of **feedback,** or input. You will get feedback from coworkers and bosses. It is important for you to learn to accept both positive and negative feedback. This input will help you learn and improve. Positive feedback is easy to accept, but negative feedback can be difficult to accept. This lesson will present strategies to help you use feedback.

## Respond Appropriately to Positive Feedback

Think of a time when you received positive feedback. Maybe someone complimented you on a task you had done well. How did the positive feedback make you feel? How did you respond to the feedback?

Sometimes you might feel a little embarrassed by praise. If so, try to avoid embarrassment. Don't pretend that you don't deserve praise. False modesty can be annoying. Try to think of positive feedback as a gift. When someone tells you that you've done well, accept the praise and thank the person who gave it. Show him or her that you appreciate the feedback.

One benefit of positive feedback is that it will help you build confidence. After someone gives you positive feedback, think about what the person said. Analyze the feedback. Figure out what you're doing right and keep doing it. Another benefit is that you can use the feedback to do things even better. Try to use positive feedback as a step toward self-improvement. In the following case study, think about which employee responded appropriately to positive feedback.

## Case Study

Tyrell and Connie work in the central receiving department of an auto supply store. They unload trucks, check in merchandise, and count the stock. They're both hard workers. Their supervisor, Megan, has noticed their hard work. In April she gives each of them an employee-of-the-year award. She speaks to Connie first. She gives Connie the award certificate.

Hard work is recognized by employers.

Megan: I know this honor usually goes to just one person. But to be honest, you and Tyrell are both such excellent workers that I felt you both deserved the award. Congratulations, Connie.

Connie: I don't know what to say. I guess I just don't think the job is that hard. I really don't do that much.

Megan later finds Tyrell taking inventory. She gives him his certificate.

> Megan: Tyrell, I just wanted to let you know that you and Connie are sharing employee-of-the-year honors. Congratulations.
>
> Tyrell: Wow! That's really great! Thanks a lot.
>
> Megan: Well, thank *you*. You're a very good worker.
>
> Tyrell: It's nice to know I'm appreciated. Thanks again.

Connie and Tyrell received identical positive feedback. But Connie acted as if she didn't really deserve the praise. Tyrell accepted the praise in a positive way. He let his supervisor know how much the praise meant to him.

## Use Negative Feedback Effectively

Sooner or later most employees have to deal with negative feedback on the job. The way they handle that feedback is important. Most people don't enjoy hearing negative things about themselves. But negative feedback can be useful. It can help employees become better at their jobs.

Use feedback to improve your performance.

If a coworker or supervisor tells you about something you are doing wrong, try to listen constructively. Listening **constructively** means listening to learn how to improve or develop. At first, you may feel defensive or upset by the negative feedback. But you need to control your emotions. If you get defensive, you might shut out the criticism. By listening constructively to the negative feedback, you might be able to improve your job skills. Accept the input and change your behavior accordingly. Sometimes you might understand the feedback but dislike the way the person tells it to you. If that happens, pay attention to the feedback. Try not to focus on the negative approach of the person who gave you the feedback. At times, you may disagree with the input. It may be helpful to discuss criticism that you do not agree with. The following case study gives an example of using negative feedback effectively.

## Case Study

Marissa is a secretary at the law firm of Reynolds, Reynolds & Farber. This afternoon she takes a phone call from Marv Tripp. He is a client who says he must speak with Gena Reynolds right away. Marissa transfers the call to Ms. Reynolds's office. Ten minutes later Ms. Reynolds comes out of her office. She is very angry.

Ms. Reynolds: Marissa, didn't I tell you to hold all my calls?

Marissa: Oh. I'm sorry, Ms. Reynolds. Marv Tripp said it was an emergency.

Ms. Reynolds: I don't care what he said. When I say hold my calls, I mean hold my calls. Got it?

Marissa: Yes. I understand, Ms. Reynolds. It won't happen again.

Ms. Reynolds didn't give her negative criticism in a constructive way. She was impolite and impatient. However, Marissa handled the feedback well. She listened constructively and apologized for her phone error. She can use the input and remember to listen carefully to any instructions that are given to her.

Your coworkers and bosses supply feedback to correct or appreciate your performance. At times, you may receive feedback that is polite. At other times you may receive feedback that is impolite. It is up to you to use that input to the greatest benefit. Use positive feedback or praise to help you build confidence. Use negative feedback to help you identify skills you need to improve.

# Comprehension Check

Complete the following exercises. Refer to the lesson if necessary.

**A. List two benefits of positive feedback.**

1. _____

2. _____

**B. When someone gives you positive feedback, what should you do?**

_____

**C. What are three things you should do when receiving negative feedback?**

1. _____

2. _____

3. _____

**D. Complete each sentence. Circle the letter in front of the answer.**

1. When someone gives you positive feedback, you should

   a. accept the praise.
   b. pretend you don't deserve the praise.
   c. tell the person about all your other good qualities.

2. When you receive negative feedback, you should

   a. use it to improve your performance.
   b. pretend you don't understand.
   c. let the other person know that you're unhappy.

3. If someone gives you negative feedback in an impolite way, you should

   a. tell the person giving you feedback that you don't appreciate his or her rudeness.
   b. be polite yourself and use the feedback to figure out how to improve.
   c. listen to the feedback, but don't change your performance because of it.

## Making Connections

Answer the questions following each case. Then talk about your answers with your partner or group.

**Case A**

Andy is a remittance processing clerk at Underwood National Bank. He and the members of his department process the checks deposited by bank customers. They organize the deposits and enter the check amounts into a computer. Then they photocopy each check. Another department in the bank double-checks their work. The head of the other department, Michelle, has noticed that Andy's department has made some big math errors lately. During her break she talks to Andy.

Michelle: I've been wanting to talk to you. Your department has made some big errors in the check tally over the past couple of weeks. You might want to talk with your team about it.

Andy: What errors? Nobody told me about any errors.

Michelle: Well, I'm telling you now. I don't want to upset you. I just want you to be aware of the problem. Here are copies of the statements where errors occurred.

Andy: Just what are you trying to say?

Michelle: I'm telling you we've found a lot of errors. After you talk to your team, please let me know what you find out.

Andy: Fine. I'll talk to them.

1.  Do you think Andy handled Michelle's feedback well? Why or why not?

   _____

   _____

2.  Would you have done anything differently if you were Andy? Explain your answer. How do you think Michelle will feel about Andy from now on?

   _____

   _____

**Case B**

Bethany is a designer for the window displays at Powell's Department Store. The store has had many compliments on Bethany's designs. But some of Bethany's coworkers have been complaining. They have told Bethany's supervisor, Jackson, that Bethany leaves a mess wherever she works. The other employees have to clean up after her. They all like Bethany and some of them have tried to talk to her about the problem. But Bethany pays no attention to them. Jackson agrees to talk to Bethany about the problem.

Jackson: Hi, Bethany. Listen, I'd like to talk to you. First, I want to tell you that we've had a lot of compliments on your window displays lately.

Bethany: Well, that's good to hear.

Jackson: The other thing I need to tell you isn't so good. Some of your coworkers have told me that you don't clean up after yourself when you finish your artwork. They've even found open cans of paint lying around.

Bethany: I guess I've been a little careless. Sometimes I just get so wrapped up in what I'm doing, I forget about details like cleanup.

Jackson: Cleanup is an important part of your job.

Bethany: You're right. It won't be a problem again. Thanks for letting me know.

Do you think Bethany handled the feedback well? Why or why not?

_____

_____

### ACT IT OUT

Work with a partner. Take turns being a supervisor and an employee. The supervisor gives the employee negative or positive feedback and the employee reacts. Discuss what each of you could do to handle feedback more effectively.

# Think and Apply

How well do you use the skills in this lesson? Complete these exercises.

**A. Think about what you learned in this lesson and answer the questions. Share your answers with your partner or your class.**

1. Think about a time when someone gave you positive feedback. Did you act like you didn't deserve the praise? Did you thank the person? Did your work improve because of the praise?

   _____

   _____

2. Ask a friend, parent, or mentor to give you feedback about yourself. Ask this person to comment on how well you perform a task or how often you are on time for appointments. Tell your friend to give you positive feedback as well as negative feedback. How did you respond to the feedback?

   _____

   _____

**B. Review your answers to A. Complete the checklist. Then answer the questions that follow.**

1. Read the list of skills. Check the boxes next to your strengths.

   ☐ thanking people for positive feedback

   ☐ listening constructively to feedback

   ☐ staying calm when I'm getting feedback

   ☐ using feedback to improve my performance

   ☐ discussing negative feedback that I disagree with

2. Do you want to improve any of your skills? Which ones?

   _____

3. How do you plan to improve the skills you listed in question 2?

   _____

   _____

# Building a Positive Self-Image

How do you feel about your work skills and performance?

Are you confident?

How do your feelings about yourself affect your work?

A positive self-image is a key to personal development in the workplace.

Your **self-image** is made of your feelings about yourself. Your self-image is related to your values. **Values** are your beliefs about what is good and what is bad. If you have a positive self-image, it means that your self-image and your values match. For example, suppose that you value honesty and consider yourself to be an honest person. In that case, you are likely to have a positive self-image. Suppose that you value self-discipline, but don't consider yourself to be as self-disciplined as you would like. In that case, you are likely to have a somewhat negative self-image. Of course, your self-image may be mixed. There may be some things about yourself that you like and others that you don't like.

The first step toward building a positive self-image is identifying your strengths and weaknesses. Second, make the most of your strengths. Then, work on improving your weaknesses. This lesson will help you concentrate on building a positive self-image for success in the workplace.

## Identify Your Strengths

Begin by thinking about your talents and skills. You can organize your skills into two categories. One category is your **interpersonal skills.** These are the skills you use to relate to others. Listening carefully, speaking clearly, and paying attention are interpersonal skills. The second category is the "hard" or **technical skills.** These are the skills that help you complete your job tasks. Using a computer, writing, and operating a power drill are examples of technical skills.

## Recognize Your Weaknesses

Make a list of your weaknesses, too. If there are some things about yourself that you do not like, then you may want to try to change them. Do not try to overcome all of your weaknesses at once. Set a goal to improve each weakness. Choose one to work on. Then make a plan for how you will improve. Expect that it will take time for you to overcome your weaknesses. Be kind to yourself while you work on this goal.

Using lab equipment is an example of a technical skill.

Be patient with the process of learning. In the workplace, you will learn many new things. But learning anything takes time. Don't expect yourself to learn something instantly. If you make a mistake or forget something, think of it as an opportunity. Mistakes provide you with an opportunity to learn. Say to yourself, "Now I will know what to do next time."

37

In the following case study, Margarita makes a mistake, but she decides to learn from her mistake.

## Case Study

Margarita works in a greenhouse. One of her job tasks is to water the plants. At first, Margarita waters the plants every day. After a few weeks, several of the plants die. Margarita's supervisor, Carlene, looks closely at the dead plants. She pulls them up out of the soil. Carlene shows Margarita that the roots of the plants have rotted. Margarita was giving the plants too much water. Carlene offers Margarita some advice about watering. Margarita takes notes as Carlene gives the advice. She says to herself, "I tried my best. I didn't know you could give plants too much water, but now I have learned something. I will know better from now on." She refers to her notes the next time she waters the plants.

Learn to do each of your job tasks well.

## Bring Your Positive Self-Image to Work

A positive self-image will help you to feel calm and confident at work. When you have a positive self-image, you will make a good impression on other people. A positive self-image will also help you to feel cheerful even when you are having a bad day. Show your positive self-image when you are at work.

Act as though you feel confident even if you do not feel confident. Try to brush off any insecure feelings and focus on what you can do at the moment. Look for opportunities to improve and build your skills. Volunteer to learn new things. You might be surprised at how people will offer new work based on the fact that you show a good attitude and a positive self-image.

You can develop a positive self-image at work by thinking about the reasons why your job is important in the company or in your community. Are you helping others in some way? Are you helping to make important materials that people need? Do you provide a vital health or social service to people in the community? Take pride in the work that you do. Read the following case study for an example of showing a positive self-image at work.

## Case Study

Horace is an apprentice carpenter. André is an experienced carpenter. This week André is teaching Horace how to build walls inside a new house. At the beginning of the week, Horace is frustrated. The nails are going in crooked. He cannot keep up with André. He starts to think that he is not doing his job very well and that André is not happy with his work. Horace becomes nervous. He stops for a moment, and tries to think positively. He likes building houses. He can ask André for help if necessary. He calms himself. Over the next few days, his work improves. André praises his work. By the end of the week, Horace looks at the work. He has built half of the interior walls himself.

Horace understands that he needs to bring a positive focus to his work. By thinking in negative ways, Horace starts to doubt himself. But he finds a way to get back on track. Like Horace, you need to remind yourself to bring a positive self-image to work and maintain it as much as possible.

Have you ever dropped a rock into a puddle? If you have, you know that ripples spread out across the water from the point where you dropped the rock. Building a positive self-image takes longer than dropping a rock into a puddle. But, like the rock in the puddle, a positive self-image creates a ripple effect. When you have a positive self-image, it makes you feel calm. This calm feeling affects all the other parts of your life. It will not only make you a more confident worker—it will make you a more confident person.

# Comprehension Check

Complete the following exercises. Refer to the lesson if necessary.

**A. Name two things that make up your self-image.**

    1. _____

    2. _____

**B. List three steps for building a positive self-image.**

    1. _____

    2. _____

    3. _____

**C. Mark the following statements T (True) or F (False).**

_____ 1. An example of an interpersonal skill is your ability to use a computer.

_____ 2. A technical skill is a soft skill.

_____ 3. If you concentrate on being a good listener, you are practicing an important interpersonal skill.

_____ 4. If you bring a positive self-image to work, you may be given the opportunity to learn new job tasks.

**D. Complete each sentence. Circle the letter in front of the answer.**

1. If you have a positive self-image,

    a. your self-image has nothing to do with your values.

    b. your self-image and your values are different.

    c. your self-image and your values match.

2. If you make a mistake at work, you should

    a. learn from what happened.

    b. have a negative self-image.

    c. stop trying to improve.

Answer the questions after each case study. Then talk about your answers with your partner or group.

### Case A

George is a clerk in a courthouse. His job includes making copies, typing, and filing. George is very good at his work. He is being trained to use the computer system. George does not feel very confident about using a computer. He is afraid that he will make a mistake.

George's supervisor, Shanice, has never considered promoting George to a more responsible position. She knows George does good work. But she doesn't think that George is interested in learning anything new. Because Shanice has never promoted George, George draws his own conclusions about his future. He believes that he will never advance. He thinks that he must be making too many mistakes in his work.

What advice would you give to George?

_____

_____

### Case B

Cassandra works in a pharmacy. She makes sure there is enough medicine on the shelves. She checks expiration dates to make sure that the medicine is still effective. She also fills some prescriptions. When she fills prescriptions, Cassandra must be very careful, even though the pharmacist will check her work. Cassandra often thinks about how many people are depending on her for their medication. Cassandra is studying to be certified as a pharmacist technician, so she asks the pharmacist a lot of questions. Even at the end of a long day, Cassandra is cheerful and enthusiastic about her work.

Do you think that Cassandra has a positive self-image? Why or why not?

_____

_____

## Case C

Marvin works the last shift at night in a coffee shop. The coffee shop closes at 10 o'clock. One evening, some customers are sitting in a booth eating doughnuts at 10 o'clock. Marvin decides not to disturb them. He puts the "Closed" sign out, but leaves the door unlocked. He will lock it when the customers leave. In the meantime, Marvin starts to clean the display case. He takes the doughnuts and pastries out of the case and starts dumping them into a large garbage can. The coffee shop only sells baked goods that have been made fresh that day.

Marvin's boss, Akele, pulls Marvin aside. "Don't EVER throw away doughnuts while customers are in the store!" she whispers angrily. "You're telling them that what they just bought is garbage!"

How would you advise Marvin to think about the mistake that he has made?

_____

_____

### TALK IT OUT

Work with a small group. Tell the group about someone you admire. Explain to the group why you admire this person. Then, talk about the person with the group. List some strengths of the person you admire. Also list some obstacles the person you admire has overcome in his or her life.

# Think and Apply

How well do you use the skills in this lesson? Complete these exercises.

**A. Think about what you learned in this lesson and answer the questions. Share your answers with your partner or your class.**

1. Are you usually in a good mood? Do you laugh at your mistakes? Do you enjoy being alone with yourself? Do you like to try new things? Think about these questions. Then, describe yourself.

   _____

   _____

2. During the next week, volunteer to do something that you have never done before. Volunteer to do something new at work. Volunteer to help a nonprofit organization for a few hours. Or help a friend, family member, or neighbor. Describe how doing something new makes you feel.

   _____

   _____

**B. Review your answers to A. Complete the checklist. Then answer the questions that follow.**

1. Read the list of skills. Check the boxes next to your strengths.

   ☐ knowing my values

   ☐ identifying my strengths and weaknesses

   ☐ bringing my positive self-image to work

   ☐ remembering the reasons why my job is important

2. Do you want to improve any of your skills? Which ones?

   _____

   _____

3. How do you plan to improve the skills you listed in question 2?

   _____

   _____

## Building a Network

Do you get work advice from people outside your family?

At work, could knowing people outside your department help you do your job?

A strong network can help you throughout your career.

A **network** is a group of people who help each other and give each other information and support. The people in your network help you and you help them. For example, a person in your network might give you advice or helpful hints about your job. You might help a person in your network by sharing information that person needs. Many people think of a network as a tool for planning a career or getting a job. But a network can also serve you in school or in your personal life.

This lesson will tell you more about how a network can support you and how you can support the people in your network. This lesson will also explain ways to **maintain,** or keep up, your network.

## Who Is in Your Network?

Many people make up your network. If you take a moment to consider the people you know, you may be able to figure out ways that they can help you and you can help them.

**Role models and mentors. Role models** are people you admire. You can use a role model as an example of how to do your job. If you have a close work relationship with someone like this, he or she may be a **mentor.** A mentor takes an interest in your career and gives you instructions, advice, and help. He or she may be willing to share knowledge and experiences.

**Internal and external customers.** The people you work with inside your own organization are called **internal customers.** People you work with from other organizations are called **external customers.** These "customers" are the people who can give you the most information and help in your job. Internal and external customers are different from the type of customer who buys goods from a business. Internal and external customers need information, not goods, from you. Your internal customers might include the secretary in the accounting department and your manager. Your external customers might include the technician who repairs the office copier and the store manager who buys your company's products. The following case study shows how internal and external customers can be a part of your network.

The people you work with are part of your network.

## Case Study

Gwen is an emergency medical technician (EMT). While she waits for a call, she might play basketball or exercise with other EMTs on her shift. Sometimes she visits with workers on the late shift. She is friendly with emergency room workers in the hospitals where she takes patients.

The other EMTs and the emergency room workers are Gwen's internal customers. But Gwen also has external customers in her network. Her friend, Samantha, is a 911 operator. Samantha has explained to Gwen that 911 operators sometimes must make decisions without much information. Paul repairs emergency equipment and has taught Gwen how to care for her equipment. Gwen's network helps her to be a strong and reliable worker.

At times you will ask your customers for help, support, and advice. But remember that a network works two ways. Your internal and external customers may also rely on you.

**Family and friends.** You might not think of family and friends as part of your job network, but they can be. A friend can be a good listener. A sister who has a job like yours can provide support and advice.

## How Can a Network Be Useful to You?

Each person in your network can offer a different type of assistance to you. Make sure you understand what each person is capable of giving you.

**Emotional support and advice.** Members of your network can give you help and advice. **Emotional support** is the comfort or reassurance you receive from others. Your friends or coworkers might support you by cheering you up and listening when you are discouraged or upset.

**Information.** Your network of coworkers, bosses, and friends is a source of information to you. Suppose you are a sales representative. If you sold a product to a customer, you may need to know how that customer is keeping up with payments. A coworker in the accounting department is a resource for this payment information. In the case study that follows, a worker contacts people in his network to perform his job.

Gary works as a commercial collector for a city newspaper. His job is to collect money for ads that businesses run in the paper. Sometimes, businesses disagree with their bills. For example, a department store may not want to pay their bill because they think their total is wrong. Or they may think that the ad did not appear in the paper as often as it should have. Gary must be in touch with the accounting department and sometimes the sales department. He must find out if mistakes were made in the billing. He needs to work with the sales department to find out the number of days the ad should have appeared. These coworkers are part of his network.

You can also learn valuable career information from people in your network. If you are planning your career, you might ask friends and family about different jobs. Suppose you are interested in a career in health care. A relative or friend who works in a hospital may be able to tell you what it is like to work there. You might even find a job through the people in your network.

## How Do You Build and Maintain a Network?

Building and maintaining an effective network takes effort. Get to know the people in your department. Be friendly and helpful. Become familiar with the different areas and services of the company. You may also want to join trade and professional organizations to get to know people who work in the same industry but in a different company.

You can build your network by getting to know people in the company.

The best networks don't just happen. It takes a real effort to build and maintain them. Make the effort and you will increase your job effectiveness and satisfaction.

# Comprehension Check

Complete the following exercises. Refer to the lesson if necessary.

**A. What is a network?**

_____

_____

**B. List two kinds of help you can get from a network on the job.**

1. _____

2. _____

**C. Explain how a mentor in your network can help you.**

_____

**D. Mark the following statements T (True) or F (False).**

_____ 1. You don't need to include people outside your department in your job network.

_____ 2. A role model is a set of instructions that explains your job.

_____ 3. Joining a trade or professional organization can help you build your network.

**E. Read the following questions. Circle the letter in front of the answer.**

1. Which of the following is an external customer in your network?

   a. the receptionist at your company
   b. an order-taker at the company that supplies shipping boxes
   c. a clerk in the accounting department in your company

2. Which of the following is good at building a network?

   a. Salvy keeps a list of people he meets in other departments and seeks them out at company social events.
   b. Pierce often calls his friends at work for help and advice, but he doesn't like to return their favors.
   c. Jaqueline is frequently rude and impatient with the person who repairs the office fax machines.

Answer the questions following each case. Then talk about your answers with your partner or group.

## Case A

Audrey and Alex are entry-level patrol officers. Audrey is relaxed and friendly on the job. She is friendly with two experienced officers at the station and asks them for advice from time to time. She also discusses security and safety issues with a high school buddy who is a security guard at a bank. She is becoming familiar with the firefighters in the same district. Audrey is also trying to get to know the people who live in the neighborhood.

Alex is very serious about his job. He has a good relationship with the other young officers, but he doesn't think he should socialize on the job. He is afraid to bother the older officers. He doesn't speak to them often. In the neighborhood he patrols, Alex tries to keep his eyes open and his mouth shut. He doesn't really know much about the people on his beat. Alex thinks his job and home life should be separate. So he doesn't tell his wife much about what goes on at work.

Describe some differences between Audrey's network and Alex's network.

_____

_____

_____

_____

## Case B

Sharon is an aerobics instructor who has taught at several health clubs. She knows many instructors. She makes an effort to learn the faces and names of the students in her classes. Sharon recently completed a degree in physical education and has made friends with several of her teachers. She tries to make time to help the PTA at her daughter's school. She is close to her sister and brother, who live in the same area.

1. List the people in Sharon's network.

_____

_____

_____

2. How might each person help Sharon?

_____

_____

_____

_____

## TALK IT OUT

Work with a partner. If you have a job, talk with your partner about the people who are or could be part of your network. Discuss how your network could help you on the job. If you are looking for a job, talk about the people who are part of your personal network. Brainstorm with your partner to think of other people who could become part of your network. Discuss how the people in your network could help you as you look for a job. Then, write a few sentences describing your network. Include the ideas you have for expanding your network.

# Think and Apply

How well do you use the skills in this lesson? Complete these exercises.

**A. Think about what you learned in this lesson and answer the questions. Share your answers with your partner or your class.**

1. Think about your job or school experience in terms of the network you have. Make a list of people in your network and describe how each person supports you.

   _____

   _____

   _____

2. Did you ever lose track of someone who was part of your network? Describe what happened. How could you have kept up your connection with that person?

   _____

   _____

**B. Review your answers to A. Complete the checklist. Then answer the questions that follow.**

1. Read the list of skills. Check the boxes next to your strengths.

   ☐ using your network for support, information, and help

   ☐ including mentors, customers, family members, and friends in your network

   ☐ getting to know your coworkers

   ☐ returning favors and support from members of your network

2. Do you want to improve any of your skills? Which ones?

   _____

3. How do you plan to improve the skills you listed in question 2?

   _____

# Lesson 7

## Dealing with Stress

How do you define stress?

Are you under a lot of stress right now?

How do you deal with your stress?

If you control your stress, you can make it work for you on the job.

**Stress** is tension. Stress can make you feel anxious, angry, or upset. As a result, stress makes it harder to get work done. Imagine that you are in a job interview. The interviewer asks you, "How do you deal with stress?" What would you say? Your answer is important because every job contains some level of stress. This lesson will explain different types of stress and ways to control the stress.

### Avoid Deadline Stress

Have you ever had too much work to do and not enough time in which to do it? If so, then you have felt deadline stress. A **deadline** is a time when something must be done. Deadline stress occurs when you fear that you will not finish your task on time. To deal with deadline stress, try to let go of your fear of not meeting your deadline. Instead, focus on ways to meet the deadline. Following are some tips to help you deal with deadline stress.

**Do one thing at a time.** Don't let your deadline distract you from your work. Concentrate on your work. Break a big job into smaller tasks. Plan your work with your deadline in mind. Check your progress. But don't let worry about your deadline take away energy that you need to do your work.

**Know when to ask for help.** Do everything you can to meet your deadline without help from others. But if you think that even if you do your best, you may not make it, then tell your supervisor. Your supervisor needs to know if there will be a problem meeting the deadline. Your supervisor may be able to find someone to help you. Your supervisor may be able to give you more time.

## Make Stress Work for You

You might respond to stress by having negative feelings, such as anger or fear. However, negative feelings will not help you to deal with stress. Negative feelings drain energy away from you. To make stress work for you, have positive feelings about it. Positive feelings can give you the energy you need to deal with the situation.

Try to view problems as opportunities to learn.

**Change negative feelings into positive feelings.** Redefine what is fun. Say to yourself, "I am glad this happened. Solving this problem will help me learn." Or, say to yourself, "When I finish this task, people will see how good I am at my job." Maybe the most positive statement you can think of is, "I will be happy after I have met this deadline." If so, concentrate on that statement.

**Turn positive feelings into energy.** Negative feelings, such as anger and fear, make you feel tired. Positive feelings, such as happiness, give you energy. When you change negative feelings into positive feelings, you get extra energy that you can use to solve your problem. To turn your positive feelings into energy, plan your work and get started. The following case study shows how.

## Case Study

Brenda is an experienced plumber. She does not want to work with Tony, who is an apprentice. Brenda thinks that Tony will slow her down. Brenda starts to feel anxious about working with Tony. She thinks that she will have to teach him how to do everything. However, Brenda then tries to change her point of view. She begins to think positively. She tells herself that working with Tony will be fun and a challenge. Then Brenda goes on a job with Tony. She discovers that she likes explaining things to him. It makes Brenda feel good to know that she has something to teach someone.

## Control the Stress that Comes from Other People

When you work regularly with other people, you may feel stress for many reasons. Someone may disagree with you or do something to create a problem. On the other hand, you may do something to create a problem. When you have a conflict, remember that your feelings belong to you. The other person probably is not trying to make you feel angry or upset. Even if someone does try to upset you, it is up to you to decide how you will react. You are in charge of your feelings. To handle a conflict, keep the following tips in mind.

**Listen to the other person.** Try to understand his or her point of view. A **point of view** is the position from which you consider something. Assume that the other person has a good reason for his or her point of view.

**State your point of view neutrally.** Explain your point of view in a polite tone and use neutral language. A **neutral** statement is neither positive nor negative. Don't judge the other person. Don't say, "That won't work!" Instead, say "I don't understand how that will work."

**Negotiate to reach a decision.** When you **negotiate,** you discuss a problem and try to agree on a solution. Both of you must be willing to compromise. A **compromise** involves giving up something to meet a goal. Read how Kyra compromises.

When you negotiate, be polite.

## Case Study

Sally, a legal secretary, is going on vacation. Sally talks to her boss, Lena, about it. Sally tells Lena that Kyra, another legal secretary, can help Lena. When Kyra hears this, she is upset. Sally did not ask Kyra if she would have time to help. Kyra has a challenging work load because she works for two lawyers. Kyra explains her work load to Sally, being careful not to blame her. Kyra compromises by agreeing to answer Lena's phone when Sally is gone. Then Kyra says, "Please don't volunteer me to do work without asking me first. I'm glad to help, but I would need to clear your work request with my bosses."

## Use a Healthy Lifestyle to Help Reduce Stress

Some jobs cause a general feeling of stress. You may do work that is frustrating or that affects you emotionally. For example, police officers feel stress because the work they do is dangerous.

To deal with stress, make sure that your lifestyle is healthy. Take care of yourself. Eat nutritious meals. Get plenty of sleep at night. Exercise regularly. Try to make time to relax every day.

# Comprehension Check

Complete the following exercises. Refer to the lesson if necessary.

**A. Name two different causes of stress.**

1. _____

2. _____

**B. Why do you think it is important to listen to a person with whom you have a conflict?**

_____

_____

**C. Read the following sentences. Circle the letter in front of the answer.**

1. One way you can cope with deadline stress is to

   a. do one thing at a time.
   b. negotiate to reach a decision.
   c. worry more about it.

2. Sometimes dealing with another person can be stressful. When that happens, who is responsible for resolving the conflict?

   a. you
   b. the other person
   c. both you and the other person

3. Stating your point of view neutrally is one way that you can

   a. control the stress that comes from other people.
   b. change your negative feelings into positive feelings.
   c. control deadline stress.

**D. Mark the following statements T (True) or F (False).**

_____ 1. Changing your negative feelings into positive feelings will make you tired.

_____ 2. When you negotiate, you must be willing to compromise.

## Making Connections

Answer the questions after each case study. Then talk about your answers with your partner or group.

### Case A

Antonio is a flight attendant. One of his duties is to take tickets from passengers as they board the plane. Antonio must also check to make sure that each passenger is carrying no more than two pieces of baggage. Antonio sends extra bags to the plane's cargo section. Antonio is careful in his work. He knows that too much carry-on baggage can be a safety hazard.

Marcus is a passenger on Antonio's flight. Marcus is carrying a laptop computer, a briefcase, and a suitcase. Antonio stops Marcus at the gate. "Excuse me," Antonio says, "but you can only carry two bags on board the plane."

Marcus is extremely upset. "Why are you giving me a hard time?" says Marcus. "I need all of these bags."

What kind of stress is Antonio experiencing? How can Antonio work with Marcus to resolve the issue?

_____

_____

### Case B

Carmen is a library assistant. Part of her job is to read the call numbers of books on the shelves. If a book is in the wrong place, Carmen must reshelve it. Carmen dislikes this part of her job. She thinks it is boring. Also, sometimes it takes Carmen a long time to find the spot where a book should be reshelved.

How can Carmen cope with her stress?

_____

_____

_____

**Case C**

Mandy is a nurse. She enjoys her job. Lately, though, Mandy has noticed that she never thinks about anything but her work, even when she is at home. She frequently gets tension headaches. It is hard for her to sleep at night. What kind of stress is Mandy experiencing? How can she deal with this stress?

_____

_____

_____

## TRY IT OUT

Work with a group to take a survey. Write a questionnaire about dealing with stress. Include questions that relate to the lesson. For example, you might ask "How often do you try to negotiate to reach a decision?" Possible answers might include "always," "sometimes," and "never." Other questions might be "Do you eat nutritious meals?" "How much sleep do you get in one night?" Questionnaires should include about ten questions. Distribute your questionnaire to other class groups. Then collect the results. Discuss your results with the rest of the class.

# Think and Apply

How well do you use the skills in this lesson? Complete these exercises.

**A. Think about what you learned in this lesson and answer the questions. Share your answers with your partner or your class.**

1. During the next week, notice when you feel stress. Pay attention to the stress that you experience. Pay attention to how you control your feelings during stressful situations. On the lines below, name one type of stress you experienced during the week. Explain how you dealt with it.

   _____

   _____

2. Job interviewers commonly ask how people deal with stress. How would you answer this question?

   _____

**B. Review your answers to A. Complete the checklist. Then answer the questions that follow.**

1. Read the list of skills. Check the boxes next to your strengths.
   - ☐ doing one thing at a time
   - ☐ knowing when to ask for help
   - ☐ changing my negative feelings into positive feelings
   - ☐ turning my positive feelings into energy
   - ☐ listening to other people
   - ☐ stating my point of view neutrally
   - ☐ negotiating to reach a decision
   - ☐ taking care of my health

2. Do you want to improve any of your skills? Which ones?

   _____

3. How do you plan to improve the skills you listed in question 2?

   _____

# Facing Fears and Taking Risks

What effects can fear have on people in the workplace?

What role does risk-taking have in doing your job?

To succeed in the workplace, learn to face your fears and take risks.

Everyone has fears on the job. Some fears relate to matters of personal safety. But most fears are traced to fears of failure. Do I really have the skills to do the job? Can I take care of my latest task? Will I ever be able to please my demanding supervisor? Fears can keep you from succeeding in your job and career. Meeting these fears and overcoming them will help you perform your job.

## Examine Your Fears

You can take positive steps to manage your fears. Other people can help you handle and get rid of your fears, but most of the work will be up to you. You must begin by looking at your fears to see if they are **warranted,** or likely to come true.

## Resolve Fears About Safety

Fears about your personal safety on the job are important to consider. Learn as much as you can about the dangers of a job before you take it. Facing your fears doesn't mean you should take a job to overcome a long-held fear. If you are uncomfortable at the sight of blood, a job in the medical industry is probably not a good choice for you.

Learn safety procedures to overcome fears at work.

Ask your supervisor what **procedures,** or ways of doing things, and equipment are available to keep you safe. Your employer may require that you wear safety equipment in every work situation. Make the effort to learn and practice the safest way to do the job. Be sure to attend any safety classes offered by the company.

## Overcome Fears of Failure

Most fears on the job are related to the fear of failure. Everybody has suffered from this fear at some time. Did you ever **procrastinate,** or put off, writing a report because you were afraid you'd mess it up?

People often procrastinate because of fear of failure. Fear of failure can keep people from acting at all. Many people have not done their best on the job or have turned down promotions because of this fear. They think that they might fail at the new job. So they stick with the familiar job. Overcoming a fear of failure will help you develop skills and build confidence for future tasks.

Following are some strategies to help you deal with fear of failure.

- Don't think of success and failure as "all or nothing." You can be partly successful. Recognize that there are different amounts of success and failure in everything you do.

- You don't have to be excellent at everything you do. Try something you would like to do, even if you're not sure you'll be good at it.

- Define success for yourself. Don't let someone else define whether you are a success or failure. Reach for the goals you set for yourself.

- Learn from your experiences.

- Don't give up. The most successful people have had to struggle to overcome failure.

The following case study shows that admitting a fear of failure is often the first step to overcoming it.

## Case Study

Raul is a firefighter. His supervisor suggests that he take the exam for the job of lieutenant. Raul doesn't like written exams. He is afraid of failure but won't admit it. "Why should I do all that work for nothing?" he says. "Besides, I don't want more responsibility." A good friend talks to Raul about facing his fear of failure. Raul admits that he is afraid of failing. Then he works with a more experienced firefighter to make plans to overcome it. He decides that even if he doesn't pass the exam, he'll know how to do better next time.

## Take Risks to Explore Opportunities

People who take risks have a positive attitude toward challenges and problems. A **risk** is a chance for loss or harm. For example, if you take responsibility for a new job task, you are taking a risk. You are taking a chance that you will be able to accomplish the new job task. If you fail, you may not be given such a task again. If you succeed, you may be given more responsibilities.

Taking risks requires courage. When problems and challenges are new, risk-takers need to create solutions that have not been tested before. Taking risks means being creative.

## Calculate Your Risks

The best risk-takers don't just close their eyes and jump in. They examine their ideas and solutions carefully before they try them out. They use all the information they can find to **calculate,** or figure out, whether the risk is worth taking. For example, a flight attendant may consider becoming a safety trainer for the airline. First, she learns about the training and education required to become a trainer. Second, she learns that she needs to be in good physical shape. She decides to exercise more often. Risk-takers make solid preparations for their next move.

The following case study shows how a worker can benefit from taking a calculated risk.

### Case Study

Willa gives guided tours to museum visitors. She wants to take visitors "behind the scenes" so they can see museum scientists at work. Several scientists like her idea. But Willa's boss doesn't favor new ideas. "More trouble than they're worth," he says. Willa doesn't know what to do. Should she risk trying her idea without asking her boss? Or should she risk telling him and being told "no"? Willa decides it would be foolish to take visitors behind the scenes without telling her boss. Instead, she makes complete plans for her tour. Then she presents her idea to her boss. Willa has been careful to think of questions he might have and prepare answers. Her careful work pays off.

Willa thinks ahead before she presents ideas to her boss.

Facing and overcoming your fears will make you able to do your best in your job. It also will help you to confidently look ahead to personal advancement. It is the first step to becoming a creative risk-taker who can develop fresh new ideas on the job.

# Comprehension Check

Complete the following exercises. Refer to the lesson if necessary.

**A. What are two kinds of fears that you might feel in your job?**

1. _____

2. _____

**B. What can you do if you are afraid for your safety at work?**

_____

**C. List three strategies to help you deal with fear of failure.**

1. _____

2. _____

3. _____

**D. Mark the following statements T (True) or F (False).**

_____ 1. Fear of failure usually motivates people to do their best work on the job.

_____ 2. Good risk-takers are creative, but careful, in trying out new ideas.

**E. Read the following sentences. Circle the letter in front of the answer.**

1. Which of these workers is having trouble admitting his or her fear of failure?

    a. Tamara is worried about becoming a team leader in her factory. She tells a friend that she's afraid of "messing up" and losing the job.
    b. Leroy decides to have fun writing a song for the company variety show, even if his coworkers laugh at him.
    c. Margie says she was right to refuse a promotion because turning it down made her feel so good.

2. Risk-taking is often a sign of

    a. courage.
    b. fear of failure.
    c. procrastinating.

## Making Connections

Answer the questions following each case. Then talk about your answers with your partner or group.

**Case A**

Janeen works as a veterinarian's assistant. She assists the veterinarian in treating dogs and cats. Recently, the vet has decided to start treating horses. She will want Janeen to travel to farms and assist her. Janeen has never treated horses before. She is worried about her safety if she works with them.

Make some suggestions about how Janeen could overcome her fear and protect herself.

_____

_____

_____

_____

**Case B**

Jeremy is a stock clerk at a store that sells bedding, tablecloths, and other linens. He restocks the display shelves with goods from the stock room. He also keeps track of the inventory. Jeremy and three other clerks work for the manager of the stock room. Jeremy has an idea for a new inventory system. He believes the new system would make restocking shelves and taking inventory easier. But Jeremy has been at the store only three months and is afraid the manager will not like his idea. Jeremy decides to forget about his idea.

What advice would you give to Jeremy?

_____

_____

_____

_____

**Case C**

Shawn is a clerk in an insurance company. Her job is to check the forms that people fill out when they apply for insurance. She must make sure that the forms are complete. She tells her supervisor about incomplete forms or unclear information on the forms. Shawn excels at what she does. Her supervisor tells Shawn that she should take training to become an insurance underwriter, someone who makes the final decisions about accepting people for insurance. Shawn politely accepts the advice and says she'll think about it. For the next few weeks, Shawn performs poorly at work. She checks fewer and fewer forms each day. She complains that she has too much stress and decides not to get additional training.

What is Shawn's real problem? What do you think she should do?

_____

_____

_____

_____

## ACT IT OUT

Work with a partner. One of you will describe a situation when you procrastinated. It can be a home, school, or work situation. The other will play the role of a counselor and suggest possible reasons for the procrastination. Use the information from this lesson to offer advice. Then reverse roles and repeat the exercise. Discuss your findings with the class.

# Think and Apply

How well do you use the skills in this lesson? Complete these exercises.

**A. Think about what you learned in this lesson and answer the questions. Share your answers with your partner or your class.**

1. Think about a time or situation in your life when fear kept you from doing something you wanted to do. What were you afraid of? How could you have overcome your fear?

   _____

   _____

   _____

2. Describe a situation at school, home, or work where you took a calculated risk that worked out well. Describe a risk you took that turned out badly. Compare and contrast the two situations.

   _____

   _____

   _____

**B. Review your answers to A. Complete the checklist. Then answer the questions that follow.**

1. Read the list of skills. Check the boxes next to your strengths.

   ☐ learning and practicing safe procedures at work

   ☐ admitting your fear of failure

   ☐ using strategies to overcome fear of failure

   ☐ taking calculated risks

2. Do you want to improve any of your skills? Which ones?

   _____

   _____

3. How do you plan to improve the skills you listed in question 2?

   _____

# Accepting and Handling Responsibility

Accepting and handling responsibility is the foundation for all other workplace skills.

To succeed on the job, you must be willing to accept responsibility and be able to handle it. To accept responsibility, you need to understand what is expected of you. To handle responsibility, you need to show you are committed to completing quality work. You handle your responsibilities by completing your job tasks. This lesson will show you effective ways to perform work responsibly.

## Understand Your Responsibilities

Having a **sense of responsibility** toward your job means that you are aware of what must be done. You think your job is important and you are ready to do it. Employers are eager to hire workers with a strong sense of responsibility. As an employee, you need to understand your responsibilities. Ask your supervisor to clarify or explain any job tasks that are confusing to you.

## Take Your Responsibilities Seriously

You may not be president of your organization, but your job is important to the organization. You can show your sense of responsibility by the way you accept and handle your duties. You need to be willing to bear the **consequences,** or results, of what you do on the job. To help see the importance of your job, imagine what would happen without it. Suppose you are a receptionist for a doctor. Ask yourself what would happen if the doctor had no receptionist. Your answer will probably be "Confusion!" The doctor wouldn't know when patients arrived. The doctor or nurse would have to take valuable time away from patients to answer the phone, write down appointments, find records, and file charts.

## Learn How Your Job Affects Others

Learning is part of handling responsibility. You'll learn what is expected from you at work. But you will also need to think about your performance and how it affects others. Consider the ways that your work affects people inside and outside of your organization. Perform your job in a way that creates a positive effect on your coworkers and the people you serve.

In the following case study, a worker considers how his performance can affect others.

### Case Study

Curtis is a utility worker. He works with crews to install and maintain water services for people in the city. He is training to become a crew leader. Today he is learning about the use of radios. He learns that the communication between the dispatcher and the crew is very important. The dispatcher

A leader of a work group needs to display high standards.

needs to know where the crews are in the city in case of an emergency. If a dispatcher calls a crew leader, the leader must respond in a specific way. Curtis is learning that he needs to speak using different codes. He also needs to know how to operate the radio correctly to communicate with the dispatcher.

Curtis understands the responsibility he will handle as a crew leader.

## Display High Standards

Handling responsibility includes showing up for the job every working day, on time and with a good attitude. These things are part of the agreement you make when you accept a job.

It is important to be **punctual** or arrive to work on time. Not being at work can cause problems for your coworkers. Make every effort to be on time. Set your watch a few minutes ahead. Use an alarm clock. Of course, everybody has illnesses or other emergencies from time to time. In such cases, be responsible and let someone at work know your situation. Do this as soon as you can.

Also be punctual for meetings. Being punctual shows that you respect your coworkers' time. It also shows that you are responsible and meet your commitments.

Having a good attitude is also a key to handling responsibility. It can make your coworkers feel better about their jobs, too. Your enthusiasm will certainly make external customers and clients more willing to do business with you. The following case study shows how a good attitude can affect coworkers.

Luke is a lineman for an electric company. He knows there is more to handling his responsibilities than installing and repairing electrical lines. Sometimes he has to respond to emergencies. He tries to hurry to these jobs so people will have their electricity back on. He shows enthusiasm for his job even late at night in heavy storms. He quickly unloads his tools from the truck. He volunteers to carry heavy equipment. He is usually the first person to climb up a pole even in storm situations. This inspires his crew to work harder. His customers appreciate his attitude.

Luke directs his crew during an emergency.

## Try to Improve Performance

Working to improve your performance is also part of handling responsibility. Nobody is a perfect worker all the time. But making an effort to do better shows your sense of responsibility. Ask supervisors and coworkers for **feedback,** their judgment and comments, on the way you do a task. Ask how you can do better. This will help you identify your strengths and weaknesses.

When you are comfortable with the responsibility you have, you might choose to ask for extra work. Accepting more responsibility may lead to a promotion. Handling your responsibilities well will increase your confidence. Your employers will also feel more confident about you.

# Comprehension Check

Complete the following exercises. Refer to the lesson if necessary.

**A. Define a sense of responsibility.**

_____

_____

_____

**B. List two reasons why your supervisor might give you more responsibilities.**

1. _____

2. _____

**C. How can you can make yourself aware of the importance of your job?**

_____

**D. Read the following sentences. Circle the letter in front of the answer.**

1. You think that the man who works at the desk next to you lacks a sense of responsibility toward his job. What behavior makes you think this?

   a. He has a good attitude.
   b. He is frequently late for work.
   c. He is friendly to his coworkers.

2. Read the brief descriptions below. Which worker handles responsibilities best?

   a. Letitia sometimes is absent from her data entry job without telling anyone. She makes up for this by working harder when she is there.
   b. Larry is a skillful forklift operator. He can manuever the machine better than anyone in the company. He will not stay late to help with rush shipments.
   c. Jose is very enthusiastic about his job preparing food trays in a hospital kitchen. He carefully checks the trays to make sure each patient gets the right food.

Answer the questions following each case. Then talk about your answers with your partner or group.

## Case A

Warren is a receiving clerk at a factory. He often receives shipments of hazardous chemicals. One of his responsibilities is to see that the chemicals are stored safely. He has received safety training for handling hazardous materials. Warren doesn't worry much about these dangers. There has never been an accident at the company involving these materials. He follows instructions for handling them only when it doesn't involve more work. He has forgotten some of his safety training and doesn't bother to relearn it.

Is Warren handling his responsibilities? Explain your answer.

_____

_____

_____

## Case B

Tabitha is working as a server at a restaurant so that she can earn money to go to college. One morning she receives a call from an admissions officer at a college to which she has applied. He would like to interview her that afternoon, but Tabitha is scheduled to work then. She decides the interview is more important than work. She doesn't show up at the restaurant and doesn't tell anyone.

Who has Tabitha hurt by her actions? What should she have done?

_____

_____

_____

_____

_____

## Case C

Clementine works for a book company. Her job is to input corrections to manuscripts. Clementine notices a word that she is sure is misspelled in the manuscript. The proofreader has not corrected it. Although it is not part of her job, Clementine looks up the word in the dictionary. She finds that it is wrong in the manuscript. She makes the correction and double-checks the spelling. She also checks the manuscript to make sure the word is not misspelled in other places. She tells her supervisor what she has done.

How do Clementine's actions show a strong sense of responsibility to her job?

_____

_____

_____

## TALK IT OUT

Work with a partner. Each one should list his or her daily responsibilities over the course of a week. Discuss your list with your partner. Try to offer your partner better ways to handle responsibilities. Discuss your suggestions with the class.

# Think and Apply

How well do you use the skills in this lesson? Complete these exercises.

**A. Think about what you learned in this lesson and answer the questions. Share your answers with your partner or your class.**

1. Have you ever been hurt or had to take extra time to do a job because someone didn't handle a responsibility the way the person should have? Describe what happened. Tell what the person should have done to handle the responsibility better.

   _____

   _____

2. Describe a time when your behavior showed that you accepted and handled responsibility successfully.

   _____

   _____

**B. Review your answers to A. Complete the checklist. Then answer the questions that follow.**

1. Read the list of skills. Check the boxes next to your strengths.

   ☐ understanding and accepting responsibility

   ☐ taking the job seriously

   ☐ being aware of how the job affects others

   ☐ following high standards of attendance, punctuality, and enthusiasm

   ☐ putting forth a high level of effort

   ☐ working to improve performance

2. Do you want to improve any of your skills? Which ones?

   _____

3. How do you plan to improve the skills you listed in question 2?

   _____

## Preparing for Future Success

How are you valuable to your employer?

What can you do to get a promotion?

If you want to be promoted, you need to take steps to plan and meet that goal.

Most people don't want to stay in the same job forever. They look ahead to future success in their careers. They want to be promoted to more advanced positions. These positions offer more challenges and more rewards. Are there things you can do to make yourself more **promotable** or ready to be promoted? The answer is *yes.* You can also **monitor,** or keep checking, your promotability. You should start by making sure you are valuable to your organization. This lesson will present methods to help you plan for a promotion.

## Be an Asset

An **asset** is something valuable or useful. How can you be an asset? You might say "Do good work in your job." To do good work, you need to do your job the right way and on time.

Following are some ideas for becoming an asset.

- Learn what is important to your supervisor and to the company. Make those things your priority.

- Work independently. Try to solve problems before asking your supervisor for help. Don't seek unnecessary help. Supervisors usually like workers who do their job right and by themselves.

- Don't gossip in the workplace. Don't complain about your job or about your coworkers.

- Gather feedback on how you are doing. Feedback can come from **verbal** or spoken signs. For example, your boss may praise you when you've done a good job.

- Evaluate yourself. There is room to improve the way you do your job. Keep trying to find and carry out ideas for doing things better.

## Prepare Yourself

There are some more specific things you can do to prepare to advance. Look at some job descriptions for higher-level positions. If one interests you, talk to someone who is now doing that job. Try to imagine yourself doing the job. Ask yourself honestly if you could do the job and enjoy it.

Discuss your future goals with your supervisor if possible. He or she will probably know what you need to do to advance. This will also provide you with feedback about how you have been doing on the job. You may be able to tell whether your supervisor thinks you are promotable.

Find out what skills you need for your next job. Your company may provide training. Sign up for classes that will help you move ahead. Some companies help pay the cost of classes.

If possible, try to do some of the tasks of the higher-level job. Doing such tasks can help you decide if you would like the job. It can also tell you whether you have the right skills. Your supervisor may arrange for you to do some higher-level tasks. This will give him or her a better idea of your promotability. Read the following case study to learn how Lonelle prepares for her next career step.

## Case Study

Lonelle is a receptionist for a food processing company. She wants to move up to the data processing department. The job requires excellent keystroking, or typing, skills. Lonelle knows she will have to improve her keystroking speed. She will also have to master new software. Her company does not offer training, so Lonelle is saving money to take an inputting course at a local college. She decides to talk to her supervisor about her plans. The supervisor is happy that Lonelle wants to move up. By taking positive steps, Lonelle is preparing for promotion.

Listen to your supervisor's suggestions about ways you can advance.

## Check Your Promotability

Every company has guidelines for giving promotions. For example, you may need to work at the company for at least one year before you can be promoted. Check your company's promotion policy. Your supervisor can tell you if you need further education or training. Then you can start planning for a promotion. The following items can help you monitor your promotability.

**Performance appraisals.** A **performance appraisal** is a review of your work. It is usually created by your boss. What was your last written appraisal like? Are your accomplishments recorded? Review your performance appraisal and focus on skills that you need to improve.

**Your supervisor's confidence.** Does he or she let you work independently and make decisions? Are you recommended for training programs? If so, your supervisor probably trusts your abilities. Such confidence is a good sign that you are promotable.

**Time in your present job.** What if you've only been in your job a short time? You may feel ready to move up. Your supervisor, however, may think you need more experience. The following case study shows how Constance keeps track of her promotability.

## Case Study

Constance is one of ten shipping clerks at her company. She would like to be promoted to head shipping clerk. She knows she does a good job. She gets along well with the other clerks. Her last written performance appraisal mentioned her good work. Her supervisor asks Constance to manage the clerks for one week every month. The supervisor shows he has confidence in Constance.

Find out what skills you need to improve to prepare for a promotion.

Like Constance, you should check the signs of your promotability. Learn about the opportunities that are available in your organization. Monitor your progress. Then make a plan to make your next career step.

# Comprehension Check

Complete the following exercises. Refer to the lesson if necessary.

**A. List three things you can do to be valuable to your company.**

1. _____

2. _____

3. _____

**B. List two signs that show your supervisor has confidence in you.**

1. _____

2. _____

**C. Mark the following statements T (True) or F (False).**

_____ 1. You don't have to do good work in your job to be an asset.

_____ 2. A performance appraisal rates your skills and abilities and can help you plan for a promotion.

**D. Read the following sentences. Circle the letter in front of the answer.**

1. If you need additional training or education for a higher-level position, your organization might

   a. never promote you.
   b. provide training or pay part of your costs.
   c. give you a leave of absence.

2. Which of the following workers do you think is most promotable?

   a. Tina has been a meter reader only a few months, but her supervisor has praised her work highly.
   b. George works in a large travel agency sending out tickets and other papers to customers. He has just started performing additional responsibilities for his supervisor.
   c. As a hotel reservations clerk, Miko received a written job appraisal that praised the organized and friendly way she does her job.

## Making Connections

Answer the questions following each case. Then talk about your answers with your partner or group.

**Case A**

Christopher works as an administrative assistant for a social service agency. He is organized and careful. He often helps with fund-raising tasks. For example, Christopher keeps records of donations. He writes thank-you letters to the people who make donations. He helps Elaine, who is in charge of special events, with schedules and financial records. Then Elaine takes a position at another organization. Christopher thinks he has a good chance of getting her job. He is shocked when his boss, Alex, hires someone else. When Christopher asks Alex to explain his decision, Alex says that Christopher does not have the "people" skills to plan special events.

How could Christopher plan better for his promotability?

_____

_____

_____

**Case B**

Jacob is working as a server in a large restaurant. He would like to become a manager. On his days off, he sometimes comes to the restaurant to study what the cashiers do. During slow times, a cashier teaches him how to run a register and lets him practice the duties. One day, when a cashier is ill, Jacob is allowed to take her place.

Would you promote Jacob? Why or why not?

_____

_____

_____

**Case C**

Leila assembles electronic equipment as part of an assembly team. She would like to move up to become a team leader. She does careful work. Her last performance appraisal stated that she worked slowly sometimes, but that she was careful about her work.

What should Leila do to check on her job promotability?

_____

_____

_____

## ACT IT OUT

Work with a partner. Act out an employee asking for a promotion. One person will take the role of an employee. The other person will act as the employee's supervisor or manager. The employee should ask questions about the promotion process at the company. The employee can ask questions about a performance appraisal and ask for feedback. The employee can also ask about additional training or education that may be required. The supervisor or manager should answer the questions and offer advice. Switch roles and repeat the activity.

# Think and Apply

How well do you use the skills in this lesson? Complete these exercises.

**A. Think about what you learned in this lesson and answer the questions. Share your answers with your partner or your class.**

1. What have you done on the job in the last month that might make you more promotable?

   _____

   _____

2. Talk to someone who recently got a promotion. Ask how he or she got the job. What skills did he or she need?

   _____

   _____

3. Have you ever thought you were perfect for a job or award but didn't get it? Describe what happened. Why do you think you didn't get it? How could you have helped yourself get it?

   _____

   _____

**B. Review your answers to A. Complete the checklist. Then answer the questions that follow.**

1. Read the list of skills. Check the boxes next to your strengths.
   - ☐ being an asset to your organization
   - ☐ learning about higher-level jobs
   - ☐ working to get the skills you need for the job
   - ☐ practicing the tasks of the job
   - ☐ monitoring your own promotability

2. Do you want to improve any of your skills? Which ones?

   _____

3. How do you plan to improve the skills you listed in question 2?

   _____

Check What You've Learned will give you an idea of how well you've learned the personal development skills you'll need to use in the workplace.

**Read each question. Circle the letter before the answer.**

1. Terry has taken a job as a night security guard. He is worried about his safety, because he works alone. What should he do?

   a. He should get a different job.

   b. He should find out about procedures and equipment that can increase his safety.

   c. He should put his fears out of his mind and do his job.

2. Barry supervises the bookkeepers in a construction company. One of the bookkeepers, Margo, arrives late to every meeting. Barry should

   a. pretend he doesn't know about it.

   b. report the matter to top management.

   c. talk to Margo and ask her to come in on time.

3. Sally and Fred often disagree about how to organize the activities at the park. They probably need to

   a. negotiate to reach decisions.

   b. change their positive feelings into energy.

   c. get more exercise to reduce stress.

4. Joyce prefers to work on the projects she has always done in the past. This indicates that perhaps she is

   a. not a self-starter.

   b. good at negotiating.

   c. not enough of a team player.

5. Ann expects that her work will be evaluated at the next work team meeting. What should she do?

  a. She should listen to all that is said, both positive and negative feedback.
  b. She should criticize her work's weak points before anyone else can.
  c. At the meeting, she should agree with everything that others say about her work.

6. Which of these attitudes helps you have a positive self-image at work?

  a. Focus on your own work and don't pay attention to what others think.
  b. Think about why your job is important to the company or the community.
  c. Stick with what you can do well; don't volunteer to do unfamiliar things.

7. Jennifer works as a ticket agent at a theater. She would like to get a promotion to work as a set designer. Which of these attitudes would probably not help her?

  a. She should try to blend in so no one will have a reason to criticize her work.
  b. She should acquire the skills she needs for the position she wants.
  c. She should talk to other people who work as set designers.

8. Which of these statements is true of a network at a workplace?

  a. Once you have set it up, it maintains itself.
  b. People with hard skills don't need to participate.
  c. It is important to keep track of other people's accomplishments.

9. Carolyn works as a secretary at a high school. She often considers her work to be poor. What would probably <u>not</u> be helpful to her?

a. discussing her work with her supervisor

b. learning to evaluate her work more accurately

c. raising her expectations

10. Lilly would like to have more responsibility in her job as a travel agent. She should

a. do all her work well and volunteer to do some extra work.

b. concentrate on the things she does best.

c. concentrate on the job tasks that she likes the most.

## Review Chart

This chart shows you what lessons you should review. Reread each question you missed. Then look at the appropriate lesson of the book for help in understanding the correct answer.

| Question<br>Check the questions you missed. | Skill<br>The exercise, like the book, focuses on the skills below. | Lesson<br>Review what you learned in this book. |
| --- | --- | --- |
| 1. _____ | Resolving fears about safety | 8 |
| 2. _____ | Demonstrating integrity and honesty | 1 |
| 3. _____ | Controlling the stress that comes from other people | 7 |
| 4. _____ | Working with others; be a team player | 3 |
| 5. _____ | Using negative feedback effectively | 4 |
| 6. _____ | Bringing your positive self-image to work | 5 |
| 7. _____ | Researching your options | 10 |
| 8. _____ | Building and maintaining a network | 6 |
| 9. _____ | Evaluating own performance | 2 |
| 10. _____ | Accepting and handling responsibility | 9 |

# Glossary

**asset:** Something or someone who's valuable. page 77

**calculate:** To figure out. page 63

**compromise:** A way of settling disagreements. The members that disagree each give up something to reach a shared solution. page 55

**consequences:** The results or effects of an action. page 69

**constructively:** For the purpose of improving; helpfully. page 30

**deadline:** The day and time that a project must be done. page 52

**emotional support:** The comfort or reassurance you receive from others. page 46

**external customers:** People you work with from other organizations. page 45

**feedback:** Comments on your work, positive and negative, from coworkers and bosses. pages 28, 71

**follow-through:** To complete the tasks you have started. page 21

**integrity:** Honesty. Having strength of character. page 6

**internal customers:** The people inside your own organization. page 45

**interpersonal skills:** One's abilities to relate and work with other people. Listening carefully, speaking politely, and being friendly are examples. page 37

**leadership:** The ability to guide and direct others. page 23

**maintain:** To keep up. To carry on or to continue. page 44

**mentors:** People who take an interest in your career and help you. page 45

**monitor:** To watch, observe, or check for progress. page 76

**negotiate:** To talk with others to decide how to solve a problem. In negotiation, each member of the group contributes an idea and the group finds a solution. page 55

**network:** A group of people who exchange help, information, and support. Usually used to advance in business. page 44

**neutral:** Neither positive nor negative. page 55

**performance appraisal:** A review of your work. It is usually created by your boss. page 78

**point of view:** The way you look at something. It is your unique way of understanding things. page 54

**procedures:** A set of rules to follow. page 61

**procrastinate:** To intentionally put off taking action. page 61

**promotable:** Having the criteria to advance or be promoted. Ready to be promoted. page 76

**punctual:** Arriving or finishing on time. page 70

**resolve:** To settle. page 21

**responsible:** Able to be depended on. page 4

**risk:** A chance for loss or harm. page 62

**role models:** People who serve as models or examples of behavior or performance. page 45

**self-assessment:** Checking your own performance and skills. page 12

**self-image:** How you see yourself. page 36

**self-management:** The action you take when motivating yourself. page 7

**self-motivated:** Ready to act on one's own. page 7

**self-rating sheet:** A tool used for grading your own performance. Usually in the form of a list of tasks, or traits, that you evaluate. page 14

**sense of responsibility:** An awareness of what must be done. page 68

**stress:** Tension that can make you feel anxious, angry, or upset. page 52

**teamwork:** The efforts or work of individuals toward meeting a common goal. page 20

**technical skills:** Skills that help a person complete a task. Using a computer, writing, and operating a power drill are examples. page 37

**values:** A person's beliefs about what is good and what is bad. page 36

**verbal:** Spoken. page 77

**warranted:** Likely to come true. page 61

# Answer Key

For many exercises in this book, several answers are possible. You may want to share your answers with your teacher or another learner.

## Check What You Know (pages 1–3)
1. (a)    2. (c)    3. (b)    4. (a)
5. (c)    6. (b)    7. (c)    8. (c)
9. (a)    10. (c)

## Lesson 1

### Comprehension Check (page 8)
A. Answers include: you can handle your job tasks on time and well; you are accountable for your actions; you can answer for your actions; people can count on you; you are willing to accept extra tasks.
B. 1. (b)    2. (a)    3. (b)    4. (c)
5. (c)

### Making Connections (pages 9–10)
Case A
1. self-motivation; sense of responsibility
2. The salad bar might get dirty and the food might spoil; customers might not want to eat anything from the salad bar.

Case B
1. The EMTs must help to transport the patient. They also prepare paperwork, stock supplies, and check the equipment.
2. If the supplies are not in the truck, the team may not be able to help the patients. If the paperwork is not prepared, the hospital or office will not have the information it needs.

Case C
1. self-management
2. Winston can learn as much as he wants to know. He's excited about his work and that makes people want to work with him.

## Lesson 2

### Comprehension Check (page 16)
A. Understanding your work tasks; monitoring your performance; evaluating your performance.
B. A tool to rate your own performance.
C. 1. T    2. T    3. F
D. 1. (a)    2. (a)    3. (c)

### Making Connections (pages 17–18)
Case A
1. answering the telephone; scheduling deliveries; communicating with the drivers; answering questions from walk-in customers
2. She is not giving good service to her walk-in customers.

Case B
Antoine asks the customers if they understand. He asks if they have questions.

Case C
1. No. Ahmad doesn't realize that he is being insensitive to his patients.
2. Answers include: Ahmad should notice that every patient is cranky and doesn't like him. If all the patients react the same way, Ahmad should consider the possibility that maybe he is the problem.

## Lesson 3

### Comprehension Check (page 24)
A. Possible answers include: you need to take responsibility for group tasks; you need to help solve problems and disputes; be a leader and a member.
B. Possible answers include: the ability to listen; the ability to be open-minded; the ability to avoid losing your temper.
C. 1. (a)    2. (b)    3. (a)    4. (b)

## Making Connections (pages 25–26)

Case A

taking responsibility for group goals; following through to complete work that normally she would do as part of a team with Mr. Elliott

Case B

1. They take initiative by volunteering to complete tasks.
2. He should volunteer to complete the remaining task, which is to check the water supply for the area.

# Lesson 4

## Comprehension Check (page 32)

A. build confidence; improves job performance
B. thank the person; show that you appreciate the feedback
C. Answers include: listen constructively; stay calm and control your emotions; accept the input and change your behavior.
D. 1. (a)    2. (a)    3. (b)

## Making Connections (pages 33–34)

Case A

1. Answers include that Andy handled the feedback poorly because he got defensive instead of accepting the feedback.
2. Answers include that you would have listened constructively. You would have offered to work together with Michelle to solve the problem. Michelle may think of Andy as someone who can't take criticism, is easily upset, and someone who isn't very good at his job.

Case B

Bethany handled the feedback well. She thanked Jackson for the positive feedback and analyzed the negative feedback. She didn't get overly emotional, and she agreed to do better in the future.

# Lesson 5

## Comprehension Check (page 40)

A. feelings; values
B. identifying strengths and weaknesses; making the most of your strengths; improving your weaknesses
C. 1. F    2. F    3. T    4. T
D. 1. (c)    2. (a)

## Making Connections (pages 41–42)

Case A

Answers include that George should recognize his strengths and be patient with himself as he learns new things. They may also say that George should act as if he feels confident. Some students may say that George should ask for more responsibility.

Case B

Answers include that Cassandra appears to have a positive self-image. She thinks about how important her work is in the community, she is willing to learn new things, and she stays cheerful and enthusiastic at all times.

Case C

Answers include that Marvin should look at his mistake as an opportunity to learn. He should be patient with himself. He should also recognize that he was trying his best to get his work done without disturbing customers.

# Lesson 6

## Comprehension Check (page 48)

A. Answers include that a network is people that you have access to for help, information, and support.
B. 1. emotional support and advice
   2. information
C. Answers include by taking an interest in your career and giving you instructions and advice.
D. 1. F    2. F    3. T
E. 1. (b)    2. (a)

## Making Connections (pages 49–50)

Case A

Answers include that Audrey is building a strong job network by connecting with people who can give her support, advice, information, and help. Alex, despite his good relations with his peers, does not have a deep network of people he can count on. This may make it harder for him to do his job.

Case B

1. instructors, students, teachers, PTA members, sister, and brother
2. Answers include that the instructors and teachers could offer information for her career. Family and friends might offer emotional support. Students might help her do her job better.

# Lesson 7

## Comprehension Check (page 56)

A. Answers may include two of the following: deadlines, problems, relationships with other people, a stressful lifestyle or job.
B. Answers include that the other person has a good reason for his or her point of view, and that it is polite and respectful to listen to the other person's point of view.
C. 1. (a)     2. (c)     3. (a)
D. 1. F     2. T

## Making Connections (pages 57–58)

Case A

Answers include that Antonio is experiencing stress that comes from a conflict with another person. Antonio should listen to Marcus' point of view. He should explain that extra carry-on baggage can be a safety hazard and that he is concerned for Marcus' safety as a passenger. Then he should offer to check the extra bag for Marcus.

Case B

Answers will vary. Carmen should change her negative feelings into positive feelings. She should not look upon her task as frustrating. Instead, she should think of it as an opportunity to learn. By reading call numbers, Carmen learns what books the library has and where they are located. By reshelving books, she is helping customers find books.

Case C

Answers include that Mandy is experiencing stress that builds up over a long period. To cope with it, she should take care of herself by eating right, exercising regularly, and taking time to relax.

# Lesson 8

## Comprehension Check (page 64)

A. 1. fears about safety     2. fear of failure
B. Answers include learning and practicing safe procedures and talking to your supervisor.
C. Answers include: not thinking of success and failure as all or nothing; not needing to be successful in everything; following a personal definition of success; learning from experience; not giving up.
D. 1. F     2. T
E. 1. (c)     2. (a)

## Making Connections (pages 65–66)

Case A

Answers include finding out from the vet about what she will have to do with the horses, how to hold them, and safe behavior around them. She might want to work with someone more experienced with horses at first. She could find out about any necessary protective gear.

Case B

Answers include telling Jeremy such things as not to give up his idea, that he is not facing his fear of failure, that he feels better because he has taken the easy way out, that his idea brings creativity to his job, that his manager probably won't fire him for his suggestion—especially if he has support from the other clerks and explains his plan completely.

Case C

Answers include that Shawn's problem is fear of failure if she takes the step of taking more training and that she should at least try the training.

# Lesson 9

## Comprehension Check (page 72)

A. A sense of responsibility means you are aware of what must be done. You think the job is important. You are strongly committed to doing your job.

B. Answers may include because you have handled responsibilities well and your supervisor trusts you; to see if you are ready for an advanced position; to give you practice handling such a position.

C. By imagining what would happen if your organization did not have the job you now hold.

D. 1. (b)    2. (c)

## Making Connections (pages 73–74)

Case A

Answers include that Warren is not doing a good job. He seems to lack a sense of responsibility toward both the job and toward others who might be harmed by his careless handling of hazardous materials. He is unwilling to exert a high level of effort to do the job.

Case B

Answers include that Tabitha has hurt her servers—because they will have to work harder to cover for her—and herself, because she needs the job and could lose it. She probably should have tried to reschedule the appointment or find a substitute. At least, she should have called in ahead of time.

Case C

Answers include that Clementine was willing to do more than she had to by correcting the error. Her care in using a dictionary and checking other places where the word was used show that she handled this responsibility well.

# Lesson 10

## Comprehension Check (page 80)

A. Answers may include any three of the following: Do good work in your job; learn what is important to your supervisor and the company; work independently; don't gossip; gather feedback on how you are doing; evaluate yourself.

B. 1. He or she lets you work independently and make decisions.

2. He or she recommends you for training programs.

C. 1. F    2. T
D. 1. (b)    2. (c)

## Making Connections (pages 81–82)

Case A

Answers include that Christopher doesn't know enough about Elaine's job. He could have talked to her or to Alex about it and learned about the "people" skills needed. He might have decided the job was not for him. Or perhaps he would have tried some tasks working closely with Elaine to see if he would like the job.

Case B

Yes, because he takes his own free time to learn about the job and the equipment. He also finds opportunities to try out and practice the job he wants.

Case C

She should ask her supervisor about her performance appraisal. Then she should make plans to improve her performance. Her supervisor might be able to help her.

## Check What You've Learned (pages 84–86)

1. (b)    2. (c)    3. (a)    4. (a)
5. (a)    6. (b)    7. (a)    8. (c)
9. (c)    10. (a)